What Does a
CITIZEN
Do?

What Does a
Voter Do?

E **Enslow Publishing**
101 W. 23rd Street
Suite 240
New York, NY 10011
USA
enslow.com

Bridey Heing

Published in 2019 by Enslow Publishing, LLC.
101 W. 23rd Street, Suite 240, New York, NY 10011

Library of Congress Cataloging-in-Publication Data

Names: Heing, Bridey, author.
Title: What does a voter do? / Bridey Heing.
Description: New York : Enslow Publishing, 2019. | Series: What does a citizen do? |
  Includes bibliographical references and index. | Audience: Grade 5–8.
Identifiers: LCCN 2017055225| ISBN 9780766098787 (library bound) | ISBN
  9780766098794 (pbk.)
Subjects: LCSH: Voting—United States—Juvenile literature. | Elections—United
  States—Juvenile literature. | Political participation—United States—Juvenile
  literature. | Democracy—United States—Juvenile literature.
Classification: LCC JK1978 .H45 2019 | DDC 324.6/50973—dc23
LC record available at https://lccn.loc.gov/2017055225

Printed in the United States of America

To Our Readers: We have done our best to make sure all website addresses in this
book were active and appropriate when we went to press. However, the author and
the publisher have no control over and assume no liability for the material available
on those websites or on any websites they may link to. Any comments or suggestions
can be sent by e-mail to customerservice@enslow.com.

CONTENTS

Introduction   5

1   The History of Voting in the
    United States   7

2   How We Vote   21

3   The Electoral College and
    Presidential Elections   29

4   The Future of Voting   40

    Glossary   45

    Further Reading   47

    Index   48

Voters play an important role in safeguarding democracy by ensuring their voices are heard through elections.

Introduction

When we think about the duties and rights of citizens, voting is one that comes to mind right away. By taking part in anything from presidential elections to local referendums, American citizens cast their votes to shape the future of their country. As a representative democracy, US citizens vote for political leaders who then represent them by voting on new government policies and actions. Voting is one of the cornerstones of democracy, an opportunity for the people to speak directly to those in power. From city councils to the presidency, voting is how Americans come together to make their voices heard and ensure that those who lead them represent the will of the people.

Voting in the United States is one of the clearest markers of freedom and equality, so it's no wonder that the story of who has been able to vote throughout our history reflects the changes this country has gone through. Suffrage has been fought for by people of color, women, non-English speakers, and others who have faced challenges to their ability to exercise their right to vote—and each victory makes our democracy stronger.

Although we often think of voting as simple, the system we know today developed over the course of centuries. Early in America's history, only a small portion of those living in the new country were able to vote, and it has only been since the early twentieth century that most Americans have gained the right to do so. Exclusion from voting has had a significant effect on our country, with only a fraction of citizens being given a voice in how they are governed. Today, concerns about voter suppression and low voter turnout have created concerns about how to ensure democracy thrives.

The way we vote has also changed significantly over the years, as advances in technology make it possible for vote totals to be counted more quickly and with greater accuracy. Ensuring the privacy and security of votes cast, however, remains a concern for those who help organize and run elections. At the same time, it is important to make sure as many eligible voters can take part in elections as possible, which has made early voting and other accommodations crucial.

Voters do more than just turn up to the ballot box every four years; being a responsible voter requires engagement with the political system on a regular basis and knowledge on issues ranging from large to small. Although the right to vote is an important one enshrined in the US Constitution, that does not mean that responsible voters simply vote without learning about the issues. It is important that voters understand what they are voting for or against, and by assuming their representatives will be properly educated on the issues, all US citizens put a great deal of trust in them.

Voting is a right, but it is also a responsibility and duty that cannot be taken for granted. The future of democracy depends on continued engagement with a large and active voter population. That's why voting is important: it shapes the future of our nation.

The History of Voting in the United States

Voting in the United States is a treasured right and responsibility, with millions of citizens casting votes in every presidential election. Many also vote during local or state campaigns or referendums. But our system wasn't initially imagined as we know it today; in fact, it has taken centuries for the United States to reach the level of suffrage we know today. The right to vote was secured by groups like women, people of color, and non-English speakers through campaigns that challenged the status quo. These were not easily won victories; it took years of hard work to ensure Americans from all backgrounds have the opportunity to cast their vote.

Democracy in the Ancient World

The United States has long been a symbol and advocate for the power of democracy and the right to vote. Although not the only democracy in the world, the US values of equality and liberty have made it a beacon for those who believe in the importance of voting rights. But the United States is just the latest in a long history of states that give power to citizens through voting. Democratic rule has roots in the ancient world, and the United States is part of the complex and ever-changing history.

Early forms of democracy can be traced back to the earliest days of settled communities, when some tribes would make decisions together rather than be ruled by one leader. As societies developed and civilizations grew, leadership styles evolved into monarchies and aristocracies. But in some cases, councils ruled over city-states or held significant political power over decision-making. These early forms of democracy were very limited in scope but paved the way for forms of government that took into account multiple viewpoints and opinions.

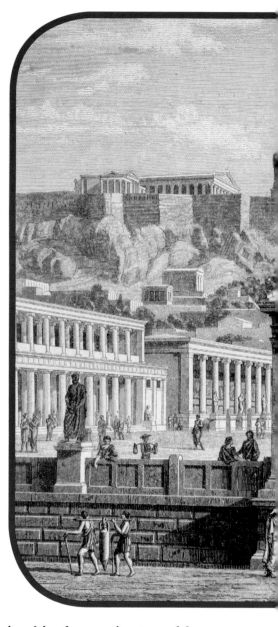

Evidence of how power was exercised in the ancient world can be unclear, so most often we think of Greece as the birthplace of modern democracy. Athens is specifically remembered for its role

Representative government has a long history, dating all the way to the ancient world, although for much of history voting rights were given to very few citizens.

in establishing the norms and values that would go on to influence democracies and governments around the world for thousands of years, including the United States. In Athens during the sixth century BCE, citizens who were given a vote were allowed to vote on potential laws. This is called a direct democracy, as opposed to our own representative democracy, because voters do not elect lawmakers to vote on their behalf.

Pericles was one of the longest-serving democratically elected leaders in Athens, and he described the political system like this according to Thucydides:

> Its administration favors the many instead of the few; this is why it is called a democracy. If we look to the laws, they afford equal justice to all in their private differences; if no social standing, advancement in public life falls to reputation for capacity, class considerations not being allowed to interfere with merit; nor again does poverty bar the way, if a man is able to serve the state, he is not hindered by the obscurity of his condition. The freedom which we enjoy in our government extends also to our ordinary life.

The overarching idea that democracy draws its power and legitimacy from the people, who take part in the system by voting, will be familiar to us today. But even though democracy appeared throughout history from the days of Ancient Rome to modern history, it wasn't the norm. After Rome became an empire rather than a republic in the first century BCE, absolute monarchy became the norm.

The Magna Carta was a historic milestone, marking one of the first times in Western history when the people were ensured a say in their own government.

Exceptions to this were small and rare, often taking place in isolated parts of the world or without continuity. The Isle of Man off the coast of England, for example, has had a parliamentary government since the late 900s CE. It wasn't until 1215 that a democratic government was established in England and Scotland with the signing of the Magna Carta, and it took another fifty years for representative government to be fully put into effect. But even so, the monarchy in England held onto near-absolute power.

For most of human history, even in states where there were elements of democracy, large parts of the populations were excluded from power. In Athens, only 30 percent of the population was allowed to have voting rights at any time, and even then only free men were given the right to vote. Such exclusion of other voices was the norm even in the United States, which was founded in part because colonists lacked a voice in political matters under British rule. But even though the United States was founded on lofty ideals, even there, not everyone was given a vote.

A Limited Vision of Freedom

In 1776, the founders of the United States signed the Declaration of Independence, a document that marked the beginning of the American Revolution and the dawn of the American experiment. The bedrock of the United States is the idea that the citizens are the ultimate source of power and legitimacy and that they grant power to the government through elections. Voting was considered a cornerstone of the new state being shaped and fought for, with Alexander Hamilton saying, "A share in the sovereignty of the state, which is exercised by the citizens at large, in voting at elections is

The Founding Fathers considered the ability to vote for one's leaders to be one of the most important parts of American civic life and enshrined it in the Constitution.

one of the most important rights of the subject, and in a republic ought to stand foremost in the estimation of the law."

But the reality of voting rights in the United States was far less equal than one might think. Only white men who owned land were eligible to vote when the country was founded, and that didn't change when the Constitution was passed in 1787. The Constitution, as originally passed, did not provide any true standard for voting rights. Voting eligibility requirements were left to the states, which decided to maintain the status quo and allow land-owning males to form the government. As a result, when George Washington was elected in 1789, only 6 percent of the total US population was able to vote in the election that brought him to the presidency.

The first significant expansion of voting rights came in 1856, when North Carolina became the final state to allow non-property-owning white males to vote. It marked the first time in the United States when all white male citizens were eligible to vote, though women and people of color were still barred from the polls, as well as non-English speakers and indigenous populations.

Women's Suffrage

Another great victory for voting rights came in 1920, when white women were given the right to vote with the passage of the Nineteenth Amendment. Women had been protesting and calling for the right to vote since the mid-1800s, holding marches and organizing conventions around the country. One of the most important was the Seneca Falls Convention of 1848, which was the first such convention on women's rights and featured advocates for both gender and racial equality. At that convention, women's suffrage was not endorsed unanimously. But at two other conventions that followed soon after, it was supported despite the radical nature of the call for women's voting rights. In 1872, Susan B. Anthony was arrested for trying to vote, and former slave Sojourner Truth was denied access to a polling booth during that year's presidential election.

The campaign for women's suffrage picked up in 1912, when marches were organized in major cities. But during the earliest

Though white property-owning men always had the right to vote, women were barred from the polls until the passage of the Nineteenth Amendment.

years of the twentieth century, women's voting rights were a controversial issue. Many thought women had no place in politics, and some women even campaigned *against* gaining the right to vote. This didn't stop the steady march toward progress, though. By 1915 an amendment giving women the right to vote was gaining support around the country, and in 1917 most states had passed at least partial suffrage for white women. But it took until 1920, when

Ida B. Wells

The women's suffrage movement is one of the great political movements in American history, making it possible for women to vote. But the movement wasn't perfect; it often excluded African American women, and the Nineteenth Amendment did not extend voting rights to people of color. But that doesn't mean that people of color were not fighting for the right to vote in the late 1800s and early 1900s. In fact, there were many advocates for equal rights who campaigned and protested alongside women like Susan B. Anthony and Elizabeth Cady Stanton. One of them was Ida B. Wells, who was born a slave in 1862. After the abolition of slavery, Wells became an activist, teacher, and publisher, speaking out against lynching, discrimination, and other racist practices. In addition to fighting for women's suffrage, she campaigned against discrimination in employment and started numerous civil rights organizations, most often in her adopted home of Chicago.

all states ratified the Nineteenth Amendment, for white women to have full voting rights across the country.

Voting: A Civil Right

While 1920 marked the end of voting rights restrictions based on sex, white men and women were the only people who could vote—nonwhite citizens were still excluded. Racial and ethnic restrictions on voting rights remained in force to varying degrees until 1965, and even today, citizens of United States territories, like Guam, are unable to vote.

The first US restriction based on race or ethnicity was the 1790 Naturalization Act. It stated that only white immigrants could become citizens through naturalization, meaning that all nonwhite immigrants were ineligible for voting rights. A series of laws starting in 1876 barred Native Americans from gaining citizenship or otherwise imposed restrictions. For example, an 1890 law passed required Native Americans to apply as if they were immigrants, while a 1919 law granted citizenship to any Native American who fought in World War I. Laws restricting Asian immigrants, including Filipino and Japanese immigrants, from becoming citizens were passed in the early twentieth century. Laws restricting who was and was not a citizen were some of the ways that the federal government controlled who could vote. By not granting certain populations citizenship, those groups could not meet voting eligibility requirements.

But gaining citizenship did not guarantee the right to vote. In 1848, the Treaty of Guadalupe-Hidalgo, which brought the Mexican-American War to an end, included a provision that granted citizenship to those living in US-controlled formerly Mexican territories, but other restrictions made it difficult or impossible for these new citizens to vote. The same thing happened in 1868, when the Fourteenth Amendment granted citizenship to former slaves. It barred any restriction of rights given to citizens, but because voting regulation is left to the states, racial restrictions were put in place.

This issue was addressed two years later with the passage of the Fifteenth Amendment, which barred the federal government or state governments from denying citizens the right to vote because of their race. In response, states began imposing tests and requirements that made it difficult for people of color to register to vote, such as literacy tests (which excluded many who had no formal education) or fees and taxes (which were a high burden on low-income families). In other cases, violence and intimidation were used to keep citizens from registering to vote or going to the polls. The Ku Klux Klan, which was founded in 1865, was one group that used terrorist tactics to keep voters away from the polls.

In the early 1960s, voting became a focus of the civil rights movement, which worked to lift legal barriers and guarantee the right to vote. In 1964, the Twenty-fourth Amendment dealt a blow to state efforts to suppress the vote, barring the use of fees or taxes to deny voting rights. The next year, the federal government passed the Voting Rights Act, which made it illegal for states to discriminate in any way against potential voters and made it possible for the federal government to prosecute violations. It marked the first time that gender and racial restrictions were not in place, and the majority of Americans could legally vote. Although cultural norms and violence against people of color attempting to vote remained

Despite having full citizenship since the end of the Civil War, people of color were still barred from voting in many states until the passage of the Voting Rights Act in 1964.

prevalent for a number of years, the law was now on the side of the voter.

Removing Language Barriers

The Voting Rights Act, followed by the Twenty-eighth Amendment in 1971, which lowered the voting age to eighteen, ushered in the modern voting era. It opened up doors for millions of people who had previously been barred, either legally or practically, from voting, and it expanded what democracy means for the United States.

But there were still logistic issues that made voting difficult. One of the most important was the printing of voting materials. For most of history, all voting materials were printed only in English, making it impossible for voters who did not read or speak English to vote confidentially. In 1975, an amendment to the Voting Rights Act made it mandatory for voting materials, such as ballots and instructions, to be printed in languages other than English, making it possible for many citizens to vote for the very first time.

Ensuring that voting is possible for everyone has been the primary focus of efforts to reform the way we vote in recent years. In 1993, it became possible to register to vote at the Department of Motor Vehicles. Today, online registration and early voting are designed to make it easier for eligible voters to take part in the democratic process. It shows that while voting began as a right enjoyed only by a small few, today we understand that all voices have to be heard in order for democracy to work.

How We Vote

There are many kinds of elections and matters on which people vote around the country, ranging from local referendums to national presidential elections. All of these votes are important and shape the future of our communities. The voting process is designed to be simple and straightforward, but what does it look like? In this chapter, we'll learn more about who is eligible to vote, how votes are cast, and the kinds of issues on which voters can have their say.

Who Can Vote?

People who live in the United States don't automatically get to vote. To be eligible to vote, that person has to be a US citizen and be at least eighteen years old before election day. Anyone under investigation for, or previously charged with, a felony conviction is ineligible in most states, although reforms on such policies are being advocated for around the country.

In order to vote, first-time voters have to register, a process that differs by state but usually involves filling out a form that indicates the person's Social Security number, address, and other basic information. Some states require voters to register with a political party, while others allow for general registration without party affiliation. For those who live overseas, it is most often possible to register as a voter in the state where they previously lived without having to maintain a residence there. Other requirements differ by state, including the timeframe within which a person has to register if they plan to vote in an upcoming election.

How to Cast a Ballot

Once registered, voters are eligible to vote in any election or referendum taking place in their precinct. Every voter is assigned a polling place, where they report to cast their ballots. This can take place on a specific day or over the course of multiple days if a particular jurisdiction has early voting. It can also vary depending on party registration; some primaries or caucuses take place in different locations, depending on the political party.

Casting a ballot usually takes just a few minutes, although, if their polling place is busy, a voter may wait in line for may hours before getting a chance to do so. Long lines don't mean voters can't participate, because all polling places are required to stay open until the last person in line has voted. This is an important thing for all voters to know, since long waits can deter them from the polls.

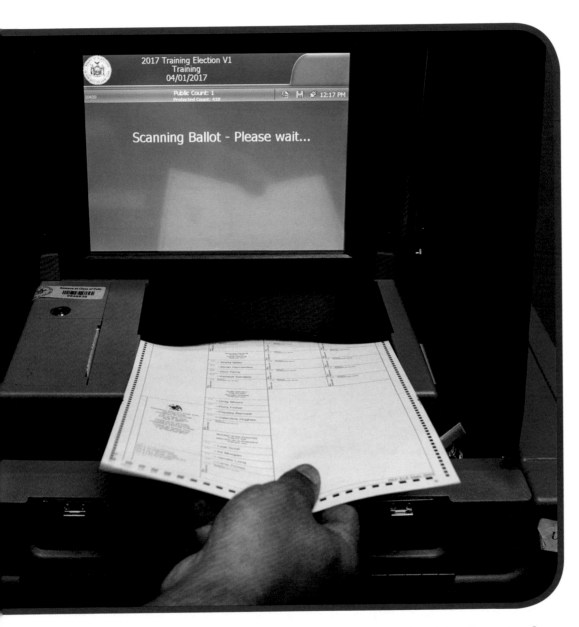

New technology is changing the way we vote and making it easier for us to do so.

What Does a Voter Do?

Once inside, voters are asked to provide their name and, perhaps, their voter registration card. Some states have introduced legislation that require a state ID in order to vote. These bills have been the source of much controversy and legal battle. After signing in, the voter is given a ballot to fill out. These ballots differ depending on where and what people are voting on; sometimes presidential ballots include local initiatives and congressional

Voter turnout is an important issue, and many advocates say the United States should make it easier for all citizens to vote in national and local elections.

Special Elections

Most elections and campaigns are held on a regular schedule. Every four years we vote for president, while congressional elections are held every two years, although not every seat is up for reelection at any given time. Sometimes a special election is called to fill a position, and those can take place at any time of the year. Special elections can be called for a variety of reasons. If an official passes away or resigns before his or her term in office is finished, a special election is called to fill the seat. A special election may also be called to fill a seat after the person who holds it accepts a nomination to a different position, such as a when a congressperson or senator is named as a member of the president's cabinet. Special elections are often a little different than regular elections; they take place in a limited timeframe and often pit lesser-known candidates against one another. These elections can also greatly change the political landscape, changing the breakdown of legislative bodies at the state or national level well ahead of regular voting.

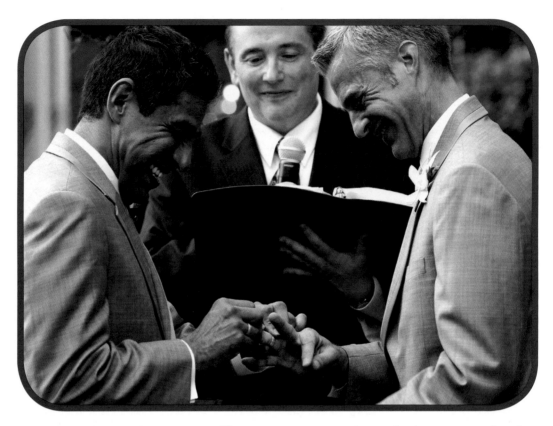

Many progressive causes, like same-sex marriage, have won in local politics before becoming federal mandates, a reflection of how important it is to take part in all local elections.

candidates. In order for their vote to count, voters need to clearly mark their choices in each category. They may leave any category blank or write-in their own choices in the provided space. If the ballot is improperly marked or altered in any other way, it will not be counted.

Once the ballot has been filled out, the voter deposits it as instructed by voting officials. This could be in a simple box or in an electronic machine that tallies alll votes cast. Some voters will even have the option of voting on a machine, rather than via a paper ballot, although the option of using a paper ballot is always available. After formally casting their ballots, all voters are given a sticker. It is a popular way for voters to show that they have done their civic duty.

What We Vote On

Voters weigh in on a range of topics and candidates, ranging from local or state officials to the presidency. But they also vote on ballot initiatives and referendums, which can lead directly to policy changes. As a representative democracy we most often elect officials who legislate on our behalf. But many states and communities have means by which residents can vote directly on proposals. This may include tax increases that affect public schools or social policy. Marriage equality legislation began as state-level ballot initiatives before being made legal across the country.

These local level votes are just as important as presidential or congressional elections. The issues and candidates voters cast ballots on shape communities on a personal level; mayors or governors have a significant impact on the day-to-day lives of their constituents. Other positions, such as city councillors, school board members, and even positions like dog catchers, give the public the chance to vote for change or affirm their confidence at all levels of government. Voting on policy changes and proposals is also an important way for voters to take an active role in deciding what kind of community they want to live in—it's democracy at its most pure, with the voice of the people dictating how they are governed and according to which laws.

What Does a Voter Do?

The way people vote and the issues on which people vote vary by state, county, and even city, so it is difficult to talk about the voting system broadly. Any given year, campaigns and votes are taking place around the country, for local or national seats. Every one of these votes is important, and it is equally important that voters understand what they are voting for. This is true of votes specific to their communities or those that impact national politics. Voting shapes the future of our country, our states, and our communities through decisions large or small, but all are linked to the ongoing power of the people.

The Electoral College
and
Presidential Elections

Voting for president is one of the hallmarks of our democracy. It is one of the most highly visible displays of our voting rights, and it routinely has the highest voter turnout for any kind of election held across the country. Presidential elections are complex, with restrictions and guidelines in place to ensure voting is done fairly and without undue influence. But the voting process is also complex, even though efforts have been made to ensure casting ballots can be done more efficiently than ever before. Casting a ballot is just the first step in the journey to electing the leader of the United States.

Presidential Campaigns

Presidential elections are held every four years, but the election cycle starts far ahead of the election itself. Candidates often begin campaigning at least one year before a presidential election is held, and speculation on who might run for the office starts almost as soon as an election is over. Candidates announce their campaigns

The Electoral College, which was put in place shortly after the founding of America, has become a source of controversy in recent years.

so early for a number of reasons, such as fund-raising and the chance to get their message to the public. But the long-term campaigning can also have an adverse effect on voters by giving them "election fatigue," which occurs when voters are tired of hearing about an election before it even takes place.

Presidential campaigns don't immediately pit candidates from different parties against one another. In fact, early on in the election cycle, candidates campaign against members of their own party to secure the party's nomination. Anyone can run for president, so long as they are born as US citizens, over the age of thirty-five, and have lived in the United States for fourteen years by the time of the election. All political parties have a different way of choosing their candidate, but the Republican and Democratic parties follow a similar process.

Line of Succession

What happens when a president is unable to finish his or her term? A president leaving office early is rare, but can take place for a range of reasons, including death or impeachment. When that happens, the line of succession is used to determine who will take the presiden't place. Enacted in 1792, the Presidential Succession Act states the line of succession designed to ensure continuity at the highest levels of government. Should the president be unable to serve, the vice president would take his or her place. But the line doesn't end there. After the vice president is the Speaker of the House of Representatives, the president of the Senate, the secretary of state, and the secretary of the treasury. The line of succession includes up to seventeen people, mostly made up of the president's own cabinet, and they all must meet the same eligibility requirements as the president in order to serve if called upon. This long list of people is meant to protect the country from going without a leader for any period of time, with the next being sworn in almost immediately after the president leaves office.

After President Richard M. Nixon resigned in 1974, his vice president, Gerald Ford, became the thirty-eighth president of the United States.

What Does a Voter Do?

Voters registered with either party go to the polls several months ahead of the presidential election to vote for their preferred candidate. The parties decide at a state level how to hold these early votes; some have a straightforward primary while others have caucuses, a process by which delegates are assigned to candidates based on how many voters at the caucus vote for them.

After the primaries and caucuses, the political parties hold large conventions with delegates from across the country. There the delegates formally declare who won each state, and whoever has the most delegates at the convention becomes the presidential candidate. These conventions are multi-day events where vice presidential candidates are announced, the party platform is formalized, and speeches and meetings are held on issues around the country. Although they often take place several months after the campaign cycle first began, these conventions are meant to give new energy and support to the candidates who then must face each other.

Following the conventions, all candidates begin focusing on their opponents. They take part in debates and run ads trying to convince voters that they should be elected to office. But their activities are restricted in some ways. Campaign finance laws require disclosure of all donors to a political campaign, and the laws limit how much donors can give to any candidate. Network television is also required to give equal airtime to each candidate, ensuring that no one candidate receives undue attention. The months between the conventions and the election itself are often an overwhelming time, with news coverage and ad campaigns running almost

Debates are one way in which candidates, be it for president or city council, can connect with voters to share their platforms and policies.

constantly. But it all leads up to one day in early November, when the people finally cast their ballots.

Going to the Polls

Presidential elections are held on the first Tuesday following the first Monday in November. This seemingly strange way of planning elections was introduced in 1845, when Congress passed a law designed to ease any possible burden on farmers who might have a hard time getting to the polls. Today, early voting means it is possible for voters to cast their ballots in the days or weeks leading up to the official voting day, and absentee ballots are sometimes counted in the days following the formal election. But for those who wait to vote on election day itself, months and even years of anticipation build to that one specific day.

Voters are given ballots by poll workers, which they then fill out in private and cast as their local election authority requires. Depending on where voters cast their ballots, they may vote on more than just a presidential candidate. Congressional elections often will also be held that day, along with any local matters that need to be decided. This makes it easier to ensure the most possible voters will weigh in, by not requiring multiple trips to the polling place.

Holding more than one vote during election day can also help overcome one of the United States' most persistent voting issues: voter turnout. Presidential elections routinely have the highest voter turnout rate of any vote in the country. Whereas in local elections, around a quarter of all eligible voters turn up to vote, during presidential elections around 55 percent to 65 percent of voters cast their ballots. This rate of turnout is low for democratic states, and introducing early voting and other measures is meant to increase it. But some feel the current initiatives don't go far enough; people have proposed online voting (though cybersecurity issues hold such initiatives back) or making election day a national holiday so that more people are off work during voting hours.

Voters cast their ballots at polling places close to their homes, assigned based on where they live.

The Electoral College

Once their votes are cast, most voters are free to watch the election results come in. But the voting process has actually only started, because the United States uses an indirect process by which the president is elected. We have a system called the Electoral College, which is the body that elects the next president of the country.

The Electoral College was introduced in 1787, and it was intended to help smaller states have an equal say in elections. Under the Electoral College system, delegates from each state meet in December to formally cast their votes for the president. Who they vote for is determined by the vote totals in their home states; some states have a "winner-take-all" system, under which whatever candidate wins the popular vote receives all that state's Electoral College votes. Other states designate a number of votes in the Electoral College based on vote totals. In order to be named president, a candidate must receive a majority of the 538 votes cast in the Electoral College, or over 270. If no candidate secures a majority, then Congress votes for the next president.

The Electoral College is controversial. Some feel it is outdated, a product of a time when directly voting for president would take too much time because of the manual counting of votes. Others feel it gives some states too much power or fails to adequately reflect the will of the people by requiring entire states with complex voting patterns to support just one candidate. Although rare, it is possible for a candidate to win the popular vote, which is determined by the direct ballots cast by voters, but lose the Electoral College.

Presidential elections have come to represent the voting system in the United States; they are important, complex, and a moment

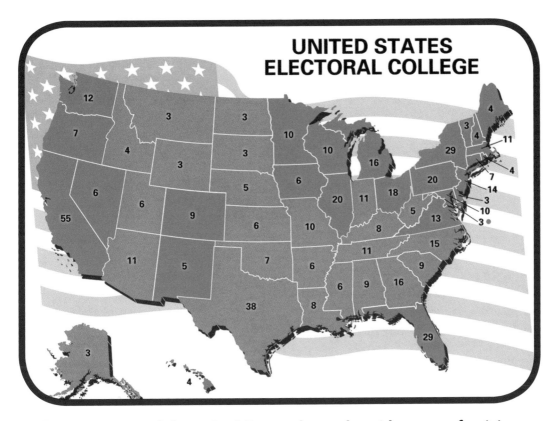

UNITED STATES ELECTORAL COLLEGE

The voting map of the United States shows the wide range of opinions across the country. The electoral votes possessed by each state play a major role in electing candidates and shaping the US government.

when the people determine the future of the country as a whole. The system is far from perfect. In that way, presidential elections can also represent voting in the United States—constantly changing and finding new ways to ensure the will of the people is carried out.

The Future of Voting

As we've seen, voting in the United States has changed with time. Although the right to vote has always been an important bedrock on which our democracy rests, who can vote and how we do so has evolved over the course of centuries, and it continues to evolve today. The way we vote now is very different from how we did a century ago, and a century from now the system will likely look very different from the one we know today. This kind of evolution is crucial to ensure voting remains fair, representative, and effective.

Getting More People to the Polls

Although racial and gender restrictions on voting have been done away with, advocates are concerned that voting laws and practices effectively exclude too many voters. There are many reasons someone can be unable to vote, and advocates are working to overcome each and every boundary that remains between eligible voters and the polls.

Staying Informed

Voting is important, and learning how to engage with democracy is crucial for young people. But so is staying informed, so that when it comes time to cast a ballot you have a full understanding of the issues at hand. Staying up to date on current affairs can sound intimidating, but all it takes is curiosity and a willingness to make time for things you care about. Staying informed can take on many forms; you can read the news online or in newspapers each week, find topics you care about and read up on their history, or talk to your friends and family about what's taking place in the world around you. You can also talk to local officials to understand voting in your area, the issues that impact your community, and how elected positions influence your community. Asking questions and then finding answers is an important way of being a responsible citizen, and you can start right away!

Primaries are one way candidates are decided by the political parties, with registered voters casting ballots for the candidates of their choice.

One of the most significant reasons people are unable to vote is logistics. This could mean that they are unable to take time off work to vote or live too far away from a polling place. A growing movement of people has called for election day to be made a national holiday. Some ask that the government mandate protections for workers who need to take time off work in order to vote. However, neither of these proposed chages are close to becoming a reality. Volunteers work in communities to drive voters to the polls and help them cast their ballots, an important resource for the elderly or those with mobility concerns.

In recent years, the push to reform felon disenfranchisement has become widespread across the country. Since 2000, all but ten states have introduced ways for felons to regain their right to vote, or they have completely done away with restrictions on felon voting rights. In Maine and Vermont, even those in prison are able to vote. In most states, those convicted of felonies regain their voting rights after serving their terms in prison or going through the probation period.

But there are some states where former felons are unable to vote, including Nevada, Iowa, and Kentucky.

Protecting Democracy

Voting is a complex and important process and one of the most significant ways average citizens engage with their government. Making sure that all possible voters are able to take part in a safe, easy process is one of the most pressing matters facing electoral officials. Elections ensure the future of our democracy. It is impossible to imagine the way voting will look in one hundred years or what kind of innovations will influence the ways we cast our ballots. But as long as the will of the people can be expressed at the polls with confidence and clarity, American democracy will remain strong.

GLOSSARY

aristocracy A government in which elite members of society or the nobility hold power.

cabinet The heads of governmental departments appointed by the president.

city council A local government panel that controls aspects of a city's government.

direct democracy A form of government in which citizens vote on all matters without representatives serving as middle men.

Magna Carta One of the first documents outlining the rights of citizens, signed in 1215 in England.

monarchy A government in which a king or queen has authority to rule.

naturalization The process by which noncitizens become citizens of a country.

precinct A specific area in which a voter lives and casts his or her ballot.

presidential election The process by which voters select the next president every four years.

referendum A vote on a particular issue, used to determine policy by direct vote by citizens.

What Does a Voter Do?

representative democracy A form of government in which voters elect legislators and officials to represent them regarding votes on laws.

republic A form of government in which citizens are given power through the right to vote for leaders and officials.

suffrage The right to vote.

voter suppression Means and practices that are intended to keep eligible voters away from the polls.

voter turnout The percentage of eligible voters who take part in any given election.

Books

Berlatsky, Noah. *Voting Rights* (Opposing Viewpoints). New York, NY: Greenhaven Press, 2015.

Freedman, Russell. *Because They Marched: The People's Campaign for Voting Rights That Changed America.* New York, NY: Holiday House, 2014.

Kropf, Martha E. *Institutions and the Right to Vote in America.* New York, NY: Palgrave Macmillan, 2016.

Marsico, Katie. *Women's Right to Vote: America's Suffrage Movement.* New York, NY: Cavendish Square, 2010.

Websites

Vote 411
vote411.org

Vote Smart
votesmart.org

Vote USA
vote-usa.org
All of these websites provide information about elected officials, candidates running for office, voting guidelines, and legislation.

INDEX

A
absentee ballots, 36

B
ballots, how to cast one, 22, 24, 26–27

C
campaigning, 31, 34
caucus, 34

D
democracy, history of, 7, 9, 10, 12
direct democracy, 10

E
early voting, 6, 20, 35
election fatigue, 31
Electoral College, 38–39
eligibility, 21–22

F
felony conviction, 21–22, 43–44
Fourteenth Amendment, 18

M
Magna Carta, 12

N
national holiday, election day as one, 43
Nineteenth Amendment, 14
nominating conventions, 34

P
presidential election, 5, 7, 14, 21, 25, 29, 31, 34–39
Presidential Succession Act, 32
primary, 34

R
representative democracy, 10, 27

S
Seneca Falls Convention, 14
special elections, 25

T
Twenty-eighth Amendment, 20

V
voter turnout, low level in United States, 6, 36–37
voting, racial and ethnic restrictions on, 17–18, 20, 40
Voting Rights Act, 18, 20

W
Wells, Ida B., 16
women's suffrage, 5, 7, 14–17